"FOUR OF THE KINDS"
PERSONAL ANALOG ASSISTANT
ADDRESS BOOK+MONTHLY+WEEKLY+DAILY PLANNER
AND RULED+GRAPH+DOTTED JOURNAL

Personal Information	
Name	
Address	
Email	
Phone	
Others	

Emergency Contact	
Name	
Address	
Email	
Phone	
Relationship	
Others	

This book consists of;

1. Address Book: >240 contacts
2. Monthly Planner: 13 Months
3. Weekly Planner: 55 Weeks
4. Daily Planner: 50 Days
5. Ruled Notebook Pages: 1/4" Spacing
6. Graph Paper Pages: 4 Squares / Inch
7. Dot Grid Paper Pages: 4 Dots / Inch

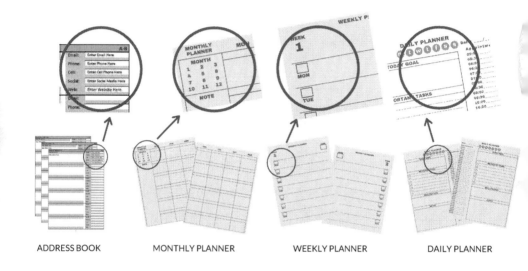

ADDRESS BOOK   MONTHLY PLANNER   WEEKLY PLANNER   DAILY PLANNER

PLEASE LEAVE A REVIEW BECAUSE WE WOULD LIKE TO HERE YOUR FEEDBACK AND SUGGESTIONS TO MAKE BETTER PRODUCTS AND SERVICES FOR YOU.

YOU ARE REALLY APPRECIATED!

HOPE YOU LIKE IT.

INDEX TO REMIND

Page	Description

TABLE OF CONTENTS

Address Book

Name & Addresses		
Enter Name Here	Email:	Enter Email Here
Enter Address Here	Phone:	Enter Phone Here
	Cell:	Enter Cell Phone Here
	Social:	Enter Social Media Here
	Web:	Enter Website Here
	Email:	
	Phone:	
	Cell:	
	Social:	
	Web:	
	Email:	
	Phone:	
	Cell:	
	Social:	
	Web:	
	Email:	
	Phone:	
	Cell:	
	Social:	
	Web:	
	Email:	
	Phone:	
	Cell:	
	Social:	
	Web:	
	Email:	
	Phone:	
	Cell:	
	Social:	
	Web:	

A-B

Address Book

Name & Addresses	
	Email:
	Phone:
	Cell:
	Social:
	Web:
	Email:
	Phone:
	Cell:
	Social:
	Web:
	Email:
	Phone:
	Cell:
	Social:
	Web:
	Email:
	Phone:
	Cell:
	Social:
	Web:
	Email:
	Phone:
	Cell:
	Social:
	Web:
	Email:
	Phone:
	Cell:
	Social:
	Web:

Address Book   A-B

Name & Addresses	
	Email:
	Phone:
	Cell:
	Social:
	Web:
	Email:
	Phone:
	Cell:
	Social:
	Web:
	Email:
	Phone:
	Cell:
	Social:
	Web:
	Email:
	Phone:
	Cell:
	Social:
	Web:
	Email:
	Phone:
	Cell:
	Social:
	Web:
	Email:
	Phone:
	Cell:
	Social:
	Web:

Address Book

Name & Addresses	
	Email:
	Phone:
	Cell:
	Social:
	Web:
	Email:
	Phone:
	Cell:
	Social:
	Web:
	Email:
	Phone:
	Cell:
	Social:
	Web:
	Email:
	Phone:
	Cell:
	Social:
	Web:
	Email:
	Phone:
	Cell:
	Social:
	Web:
	Email:
	Phone:
	Cell:
	Social:
	Web:

Address Book

Name & Addresses	
	Email:
	Phone:
	Cell:
	Social:
	Web:
	Email:
	Phone:
	Cell:
	Social:
	Web:
	Email:
	Phone:
	Cell:
	Social:
	Web:
	Email:
	Phone:
	Cell:
	Social:
	Web:
	Email:
	Phone:
	Cell:
	Social:
	Web:
	Email:
	Phone:
	Cell:
	Social:
	Web:

C-D

Address Book

Name & Addresses	
	Email:
	Phone:
	Cell:
	Social:
	Web:
	Email:
	Phone:
	Cell:
	Social:
	Web:
	Email:
	Phone:
	Cell:
	Social:
	Web:
	Email:
	Phone:
	Cell:
	Social:
	Web:
	Email:
	Phone:
	Cell:
	Social:
	Web:
	Email:
	Phone:
	Cell:
	Social:
	Web:

Address Book

Name & Addresses	
	Email:
	Phone:
	Cell:
	Social:
	Web:
	Email:
	Phone:
	Cell:
	Social:
	Web:
	Email:
	Phone:
	Cell:
	Social:
	Web:
	Email:
	Phone:
	Cell:
	Social:
	Web:
	Email:
	Phone:
	Cell:
	Social:
	Web:
	Email:
	Phone:
	Cell:
	Social:
	Web:

Address Book

Name & Addresses	
	Email:
	Phone:
	Cell:
	Social:
	Web:
	Email:
	Phone:
	Cell:
	Social:
	Web:
	Email:
	Phone:
	Cell:
	Social:
	Web:
	Email:
	Phone:
	Cell:
	Social:
	Web:
	Email:
	Phone:
	Cell:
	Social:
	Web:
	Email:
	Phone:
	Cell:
	Social:
	Web:

Address Book

Name & Addresses	
	Email:
	Phone:
	Cell:
	Social:
	Web:
	Email:
	Phone:
	Cell:
	Social:
	Web:
	Email:
	Phone:
	Cell:
	Social:
	Web:
	Email:
	Phone:
	Cell:
	Social:
	Web:
	Email:
	Phone:
	Cell:
	Social:
	Web:
	Email:
	Phone:
	Cell:
	Social:
	Web:

G-H   Address Book

Name & Addresses	
	Email:
	Phone:
	Cell:
	Social:
	Web:
	Email:
	Phone:
	Cell:
	Social:
	Web:
	Email:
	Phone:
	Cell:
	Social:
	Web:
	Email:
	Phone:
	Cell:
	Social:
	Web:
	Email:
	Phone:
	Cell:
	Social:
	Web:
	Email:
	Phone:
	Cell:
	Social:
	Web:

Address Book

Name & Addresses	
	Email:
	Phone:
	Cell:
	Social:
	Web:
	Email:
	Phone:
	Cell:
	Social:
	Web:
	Email:
	Phone:
	Cell:
	Social:
	Web:
	Email:
	Phone:
	Cell:
	Social:
	Web:
	Email:
	Phone:
	Cell:
	Social:
	Web:
	Email:
	Phone:
	Cell:
	Social:
	Web:

Address Book

Name & Addresses		
	Email:	
	Phone:	
	Cell:	
	Social:	
	Web:	
	Email:	
	Phone:	
	Cell:	
	Social:	
	Web:	
	Email:	
	Phone:	
	Cell:	
	Social:	
	Web:	
	Email:	
	Phone:	
	Cell:	
	Social:	
	Web:	
	Email:	
	Phone:	
	Cell:	
	Social:	
	Web:	
	Email:	
	Phone:	
	Cell:	
	Social:	
	Web:	

Address Book

Name & Addresses	
	Email:
	Phone:
	Cell:
	Social:
	Web:
	Email:
	Phone:
	Cell:
	Social:
	Web:
	Email:
	Phone:
	Cell:
	Social:
	Web:
	Email:
	Phone:
	Cell:
	Social:
	Web:
	Email:
	Phone:
	Cell:
	Social:
	Web:
	Email:
	Phone:
	Cell:
	Social:
	Web:

Address Book

Name & Addresses	
	Email:
	Phone:
	Cell:
	Social:
	Web:
	Email:
	Phone:
	Cell:
	Social:
	Web:
	Email:
	Phone:
	Cell:
	Social:
	Web:
	Email:
	Phone:
	Cell:
	Social:
	Web:
	Email:
	Phone:
	Cell:
	Social:
	Web:
	Email:
	Phone:
	Cell:
	Social:
	Web:

Address Book

Name & Addresses	
	Email:
	Phone:
	Cell:
	Social:
	Web:
	Email:
	Phone:
	Cell:
	Social:
	Web:
	Email:
	Phone:
	Cell:
	Social:
	Web:
	Email:
	Phone:
	Cell:
	Social:
	Web:
	Email:
	Phone:
	Cell:
	Social:
	Web:
	Email:
	Phone:
	Cell:
	Social:
	Web:

K-L

Address Book

Name & Addresses	
	Email:
	Phone:
	Cell:
	Social:
	Web:
	Email:
	Phone:
	Cell:
	Social:
	Web:
	Email:
	Phone:
	Cell:
	Social:
	Web:
	Email:
	Phone:
	Cell:
	Social:
	Web:
	Email:
	Phone:
	Cell:
	Social:
	Web:
	Email:
	Phone:
	Cell:
	Social:
	Web:

Address Book

Name & Addresses	
	Email:
	Phone:
	Cell:
	Social:
	Web:
	Email:
	Phone:
	Cell:
	Social:
	Web:
	Email:
	Phone:
	Cell:
	Social:
	Web:
	Email:
	Phone:
	Cell:
	Social:
	Web:
	Email:
	Phone:
	Cell:
	Social:
	Web:
	Email:
	Phone:
	Cell:
	Social:
	Web:

Address Book

Name & Addresses	
	Email:
	Phone:
	Cell:
	Social:
	Web:
	Email:
	Phone:
	Cell:
	Social:
	Web:
	Email:
	Phone:
	Cell:
	Social:
	Web:
	Email:
	Phone:
	Cell:
	Social:
	Web:
	Email:
	Phone:
	Cell:
	Social:
	Web:
	Email:
	Phone:
	Cell:
	Social:
	Web:

Address Book

M-N

Name & Addresses	
	Email:
	Phone:
	Cell:
	Social:
	Web:
	Email:
	Phone:
	Cell:
	Social:
	Web:
	Email:
	Phone:
	Cell:
	Social:
	Web:
	Email:
	Phone:
	Cell:
	Social:
	Web:
	Email:
	Phone:
	Cell:
	Social:
	Web:
	Email:
	Phone:
	Cell:
	Social:
	Web:

Address Book

Name & Addresses	
	Email:
	Phone:
	Cell:
	Social:
	Web:
	Email:
	Phone:
	Cell:
	Social:
	Web:
	Email:
	Phone:
	Cell:
	Social:
	Web:
	Email:
	Phone:
	Cell:
	Social:
	Web:
	Email:
	Phone:
	Cell:
	Social:
	Web:
	Email:
	Phone:
	Cell:
	Social:
	Web:

Address Book

Name & Addresses	
	Email:
	Phone:
	Cell:
	Social:
	Web:
	Email:
	Phone:
	Cell:
	Social:
	Web:
	Email:
	Phone:
	Cell:
	Social:
	Web:
	Email:
	Phone:
	Cell:
	Social:
	Web:
	Email:
	Phone:
	Cell:
	Social:
	Web:
	Email:
	Phone:
	Cell:
	Social:
	Web:

Address Book

Name & Addresses	
	Email:
	Phone:
	Cell:
	Social:
	Web:
	Email:
	Phone:
	Cell:
	Social:
	Web:
	Email:
	Phone:
	Cell:
	Social:
	Web:
	Email:
	Phone:
	Cell:
	Social:
	Web:
	Email:
	Phone:
	Cell:
	Social:
	Web:
	Email:
	Phone:
	Cell:
	Social:
	Web:

Address Book

Name & Addresses	
	Email:
	Phone:
	Cell:
	Social:
	Web:
	Email:
	Phone:
	Cell:
	Social:
	Web:
	Email:
	Phone:
	Cell:
	Social:
	Web:
	Email:
	Phone:
	Cell:
	Social:
	Web:
	Email:
	Phone:
	Cell:
	Social:
	Web:
	Email:
	Phone:
	Cell:
	Social:
	Web:

Name & Addresses	
	Email:
	Phone:
	Cell:
	Social:
	Web:
	Email:
	Phone:
	Cell:
	Social:
	Web:
	Email:
	Phone:
	Cell:
	Social:
	Web:
	Email:
	Phone:
	Cell:
	Social:
	Web:
	Email:
	Phone:
	Cell:
	Social:
	Web:
	Email:
	Phone:
	Cell:
	Social:
	Web:

Address Book

Name & Addresses	
	Email:
	Phone:
	Cell:
	Social:
	Web:
	Email:
	Phone:
	Cell:
	Social:
	Web:
	Email:
	Phone:
	Cell:
	Social:
	Web:
	Email:
	Phone:
	Cell:
	Social:
	Web:
	Email:
	Phone:
	Cell:
	Social:
	Web:
	Email:
	Phone:
	Cell:
	Social:
	Web:

Q-R

Address Book

Name & Addresses	
	Email:
	Phone:
	Cell:
	Social:
	Web:
	Email:
	Phone:
	Cell:
	Social:
	Web:
	Email:
	Phone:
	Cell:
	Social:
	Web:
	Email:
	Phone:
	Cell:
	Social:
	Web:
	Email:
	Phone:
	Cell:
	Social:
	Web:
	Email:
	Phone:
	Cell:
	Social:
	Web:

Address Book

Name & Addresses	
	Email:
	Phone:
	Cell:
	Social:
	Web:
	Email:
	Phone:
	Cell:
	Social:
	Web:
	Email:
	Phone:
	Cell:
	Social:
	Web:
	Email:
	Phone:
	Cell:
	Social:
	Web:
	Email:
	Phone:
	Cell:
	Social:
	Web:
	Email:
	Phone:
	Cell:
	Social:
	Web:

S-T

Name & Addresses	
	Email:
	Phone:
	Cell:
	Social:
	Web:
	Email:
	Phone:
	Cell:
	Social:
	Web:
	Email:
	Phone:
	Cell:
	Social:
	Web:
	Email:
	Phone:
	Cell:
	Social:
	Web:
	Email:
	Phone:
	Cell:
	Social:
	Web:
	Email:
	Phone:
	Cell:
	Social:
	Web:

Address Book

Name & Addresses	
	Email:
	Phone:
	Cell:
	Social:
	Web:
	Email:
	Phone:
	Cell:
	Social:
	Web:
	Email:
	Phone:
	Cell:
	Social:
	Web:
	Email:
	Phone:
	Cell:
	Social:
	Web:
	Email:
	Phone:
	Cell:
	Social:
	Web:
	Email:
	Phone:
	Cell:
	Social:
	Web:

Address Book

Name & Addresses	
	Email:
	Phone:
	Cell:
	Social:
	Web:
	Email:
	Phone:
	Cell:
	Social:
	Web:
	Email:
	Phone:
	Cell:
	Social:
	Web:
	Email:
	Phone:
	Cell:
	Social:
	Web:
	Email:
	Phone:
	Cell:
	Social:
	Web:
	Email:
	Phone:
	Cell:
	Social:
	Web:

Address Book

Name & Addresses	
	Email:
	Phone:
	Cell:
	Social:
	Web:
	Email:
	Phone:
	Cell:
	Social:
	Web:
	Email:
	Phone:
	Cell:
	Social:
	Web:
	Email:
	Phone:
	Cell:
	Social:
	Web:
	Email:
	Phone:
	Cell:
	Social:
	Web:
	Email:
	Phone:
	Cell:
	Social:
	Web:

Address Book

Name & Addresses	
	Email:
	Phone:
	Cell:
	Social:
	Web:
	Email:
	Phone:
	Cell:
	Social:
	Web:
	Email:
	Phone:
	Cell:
	Social:
	Web:
	Email:
	Phone:
	Cell:
	Social:
	Web:
	Email:
	Phone:
	Cell:
	Social:
	Web:
	Email:
	Phone:
	Cell:
	Social:
	Web:

Address Book

Name & Addresses	
	Email:
	Phone:
	Cell:
	Social:
	Web:
	Email:
	Phone:
	Cell:
	Social:
	Web:
	Email:
	Phone:
	Cell:
	Social:
	Web:
	Email:
	Phone:
	Cell:
	Social:
	Web:
	Email:
	Phone:
	Cell:
	Social:
	Web:
	Email:
	Phone:
	Cell:
	Social:
	Web:

W-X

Address Book

Name & Addresses	
	Email:
	Phone:
	Cell:
	Social:
	Web:
	Email:
	Phone:
	Cell:
	Social:
	Web:
	Email:
	Phone:
	Cell:
	Social:
	Web:
	Email:
	Phone:
	Cell:
	Social:
	Web:
	Email:
	Phone:
	Cell:
	Social:
	Web:
	Email:
	Phone:
	Cell:
	Social:
	Web:

Address Book

Name & Addresses	
	Email:
	Phone:
	Cell:
	Social:
	Web:
	Email:
	Phone:
	Cell:
	Social:
	Web:
	Email:
	Phone:
	Cell:
	Social:
	Web:
	Email:
	Phone:
	Cell:
	Social:
	Web:
	Email:
	Phone:
	Cell:
	Social:
	Web:
	Email:
	Phone:
	Cell:
	Social:
	Web:

W-X

Address Book

Name & Addresses	
	Email:
	Phone:
	Cell:
	Social:
	Web:
	Email:
	Phone:
	Cell:
	Social:
	Web:
	Email:
	Phone:
	Cell:
	Social:
	Web:
	Email:
	Phone:
	Cell:
	Social:
	Web:
	Email:
	Phone:
	Cell:
	Social:
	Web:
	Email:
	Phone:
	Cell:
	Social:
	Web:

Address Book

Name & Addresses	
	Email:
	Phone:
	Cell:
	Social:
	Web:
	Email:
	Phone:
	Cell:
	Social:
	Web:
	Email:
	Phone:
	Cell:
	Social:
	Web:
	Email:
	Phone:
	Cell:
	Social:
	Web:
	Email:
	Phone:
	Cell:
	Social:
	Web:
	Email:
	Phone:
	Cell:
	Social:
	Web:

Address Book

Name & Addresses	
	Email:
	Phone:
	Cell:
	Social:
	Web:
	Email:
	Phone:
	Cell:
	Social:
	Web:
	Email:
	Phone:
	Cell:
	Social:
	Web:
	Email:
	Phone:
	Cell:
	Social:
	Web:
	Email:
	Phone:
	Cell:
	Social:
	Web:
	Email:
	Phone:
	Cell:
	Social:
	Web:

Address Book

Name & Addresses	
	Email:
	Phone:
	Cell:
	Social:
	Web:
	Email:
	Phone:
	Cell:
	Social:
	Web:
	Email:
	Phone:
	Cell:
	Social:
	Web:
	Email:
	Phone:
	Cell:
	Social:
	Web:
	Email:
	Phone:
	Cell:
	Social:
	Web:
	Email:
	Phone:
	Cell:
	Social:
	Web:

Address Book

Name & Addresses	
	Email:
	Phone:
	Cell:
	Social:
	Web:
	Email:
	Phone:
	Cell:
	Social:
	Web:
	Email:
	Phone:
	Cell:
	Social:
	Web:
	Email:
	Phone:
	Cell:
	Social:
	Web:
	Email:
	Phone:
	Cell:
	Social:
	Web:
	Email:
	Phone:
	Cell:
	Social:
	Web:

Address Book

Alphabet

Name & Addresses		
	Email:	
	Phone:	
	Cell:	
	Social:	
	Web:	
	Email:	
	Phone:	
	Cell:	
	Social:	
	Web:	
	Email:	
	Phone:	
	Cell:	
	Social:	
	Web:	
	Email:	
	Phone:	
	Cell:	
	Social:	
	Web:	
	Email:	
	Phone:	
	Cell:	
	Social:	
	Web:	
	Email:	
	Phone:	
	Cell:	
	Social:	
	Web:	

MONTHLY PLANNER	MON	TUE	WED
MONTH			
1 2 3 4 5 6 7 8 9 10 11 12			
NOTE			

THU	FRI	SAT	SUN

MONTHLY PLANNER	MON	TUE	WED
MONTH			
1 2 3 4 5 6 7 8 9 10 11 12			
NOTE			

THU	FRI	SAT	SUN

MONTHLY PLANNER	MON	TUE	WED
MONTH			
1 2 3 4 5 6 7 8 9 10 11 12			
NOTE			

THU	FRI	SAT	SUN

MONTHLY PLANNER	MON	TUE	WED
MONTH			
1 2 3 4 5 6 7 8 9 10 11 12			
NOTE			

THU	FRI	SAT	SUN

MONTHLY PLANNER	MON	TUE	WED
MONTH			
1 2 3 4 5 6 7 8 9 10 11 12			
NOTE			

50

THU	FRI	SAT	SUN

MONTHLY PLANNER	MON	TUE	WED
MONTH			
1 2 3 4 5 6 7 8 9 10 11 12			
NOTE			

THU	FRI	SAT	SUN

MONTHLY PLANNER	MON	TUE	WED
MONTH			
1 2 3 4 5 6 7 8 9 10 11 12			
NOTE			

THU	FRI	SAT	SUN

MONTHLY PLANNER	MON	TUE	WED
MONTH			
1　　2　　3 4　　5　　6 7　　8　　9 10　11　12			
NOTE			

56

THU	FRI	SAT	SUN

MONTHLY PLANNER	MON	TUE	WED
MONTH			
1 2 3 4 5 6 7 8 9 10 11 12			
NOTE			

THU	FRI	SAT	SUN

MONTHLY PLANNER	MON	TUE	WED
MONTH			
1 2 3 4 5 6 7 8 9 10 11 12			
NOTE			

THU	FRI	SAT	SUN

MONTHLY PLANNER	MON	TUE	WED
MONTH			
1 2 3 4 5 6 7 8 9 10 11 12			
NOTE			

THU	FRI	SAT	SUN

MONTHLY PLANNER	MON	TUE	WED
MONTH			
1　　2　　3 4　　5　　6 7　　8　　9 10　　11　　12			
NOTE			

THU	FRI	SAT	SUN

MONTHLY PLANNER	MON	TUE	WED
MONTH			
1　　2　　3 4　　5　　6 7　　8　　9 10　11　12			
NOTE			

THU	FRI	SAT	SUN

WEEKLY PLANNER

WEEK
1

MONTH

YEAR

☐ **MON**

☐ **TUE**

☐ **WED**

☐ **THU**

☐ **FRI**

☐ **SAT**

☐ **SUN**

WEEKLY PLANNER

YEAR

MONTH

WEEK

2

☐ **MON**

☐ **TUE**

☐ **WED**

☐ **THU**

☐ **FRI**

☐ **SAT**

☐ **SUN**

WEEKLY PLANNER

WEEK
3

MONTH

YEAR

☐ **MON**

☐ **TUE**

☐ **WED**

☐ **THU**

☐ **FRI**

☐ **SAT**

☐ **SUN**

WEEKLY PLANNER

YEAR

MONTH

WEEK

4

☐ MON

☐ TUE

☐ WED

☐ THU

☐ FRI

☐ SAT

☐ SUN

WEEKLY PLANNER

WEEK
5

MONTH

YEAR

☐
MON

☐
TUE

☐
WED

☐
THU

☐
FRI

☐
SAT

☐
SUN

WEEKLY PLANNER

YEAR

MONTH

WEEK

6

☐ **MON**

☐ **TUE**

☐ **WED**

☐ **THU**

☐ **FRI**

☐ **SAT**

☐ **SUN**

WEEKLY PLANNER

WEEK
7

MONTH

YEAR

☐ **MON**

☐ **TUE**

☐ **WED**

☐ **THU**

☐ **FRI**

☐ **SAT**

☐ **SUN**

WEEKLY PLANNER

YEAR

MONTH

WEEK

8

☐ MON

☐ TUE

☐ WED

☐ THU

☐ FRI

☐ SAT

☐ SUN

WEEKLY PLANNER

WEEK
9

MONTH

YEAR

☐ **MON**

☐ **TUE**

☐ **WED**

☐ **THU**

☐ **FRI**

☐ **SAT**

☐ **SUN**

WEEKLY PLANNER

YEAR

MONTH

WEEK
10

☐ **MON**

☐ **TUE**

☐ **WED**

☐ **THU**

☐ **FRI**

☐ **SAT**

☐ **SUN**

WEEKLY PLANNER

WEEK
11

MONTH

YEAR

☐ **MON**

☐ **TUE**

☐ **WED**

☐ **THU**

☐ **FRI**

☐ **SAT**

☐ **SUN**

WEEKLY PLANNER

YEAR

MONTH

WEEK
12

☐ **MON**

☐ **TUE**

☐ **WED**

☐ **THU**

☐ **FRI**

☐ **SAT**

☐ **SUN**

WEEKLY PLANNER

WEEK
13

MONTH

YEAR

☐
MON

☐
TUE

☐
WED

☐
THU

☐
FRI

☐
SAT

☐
SUN

WEEKLY PLANNER

YEAR

MONTH

WEEK

14

☐ **MON**

☐ **TUE**

☐ **WED**

☐ **THU**

☐ **FRI**

☐ **SAT**

☐ **SUN**

WEEKLY PLANNER

WEEK
15

MONTH

YEAR

☐ **MON**

☐ **TUE**

☐ **WED**

☐ **THU**

☐ **FRI**

☐ **SAT**

☐ **SUN**

WEEKLY PLANNER

YEAR

MONTH

WEEK
16

☐ MON

☐ TUE

☐ WED

☐ THU

☐ FRI

☐ SAT

☐ SUN

WEEKLY PLANNER

WEEK
17

MONTH

YEAR

☐ **MON**

☐ **TUE**

☐ **WED**

☐ **THU**

☐ **FRI**

☐ **SAT**

☐ **SUN**

WEEKLY PLANNER

YEAR

MONTH

WEEK

18

☐ **MON**

☐ **TUE**

☐ **WED**

☐ **THU**

☐ **FRI**

☐ **SAT**

☐ **SUN**

WEEKLY PLANNER

WEEK
19

MONTH

YEAR

☐ **MON**

☐ **TUE**

☐ **WED**

☐ **THU**

☐ **FRI**

☐ **SAT**

☐ **SUN**

WEEKLY PLANNER

YEAR

MONTH

WEEK
20

☐ MON

☐ TUE

☐ WED

☐ THU

☐ FRI

☐ SAT

☐ SUN

WEEKLY PLANNER

WEEK
21

MONTH

YEAR

☐ **MON**

☐ **TUE**

☐ **WED**

☐ **THU**

☐ **FRI**

☐ **SAT**

☐ **SUN**

WEEKLY PLANNER

YEAR

MONTH

WEEK
22

☐ **MON**

☐ **TUE**

☐ **WED**

☐ **THU**

☐ **FRI**

☐ **SAT**

☐ **SUN**

WEEKLY PLANNER

WEEK
23

MONTH

YEAR

☐ **MON**

☐ **TUE**

☐ **WED**

☐ **THU**

☐ **FRI**

☐ **SAT**

☐ **SUN**

WEEKLY PLANNER

YEAR

MONTH

WEEK
24

☐ **MON**

☐ **TUE**

☐ **WED**

☐ **THU**

☐ **FRI**

☐ **SAT**

☐ **SUN**

WEEKLY PLANNER

WEEK
25

MONTH

YEAR

☐ **MON**

☐ **TUE**

☐ **WED**

☐ **THU**

☐ **FRI**

☐ **SAT**

☐ **SUN**

WEEKLY PLANNER

YEAR

MONTH

WEEK
26

☐ MON

☐ TUE

☐ WED

☐ THU

☐ FRI

☐ SAT

☐ SUN

WEEKLY PLANNER

WEEK
27

MONTH

YEAR

☐ **MON**

☐ **TUE**

☐ **WED**

☐ **THU**

☐ **FRI**

☐ **SAT**

☐ **SUN**

WEEKLY PLANNER

YEAR

MONTH

WEEK
28

☐ **MON**

☐ **TUE**

☐ **WED**

☐ **THU**

☐ **FRI**

☐ **SAT**

☐ **SUN**

WEEKLY PLANNER

WEEK
29

MONTH

YEAR

☐ **MON**

☐ **TUE**

☐ **WED**

☐ **THU**

☐ **FRI**

☐ **SAT**

☐ **SUN**

WEEKLY PLANNER

YEAR

MONTH

WEEK

30

☐ **MON**

☐ **TUE**

☐ **WED**

☐ **THU**

☐ **FRI**

☐ **SAT**

☐ **SUN**

WEEKLY PLANNER

WEEK
31

MONTH

YEAR

☐ **MON**

☐ **TUE**

☐ **WED**

☐ **THU**

☐ **FRI**

☐ **SAT**

☐ **SUN**

WEEKLY PLANNER

YEAR

MONTH

WEEK
32

☐ **MON**

☐ **TUE**

☐ **WED**

☐ **THU**

☐ **FRI**

☐ **SAT**

☐ **SUN**

WEEKLY PLANNER

WEEK
33

MONTH

YEAR

☐ **MON**

☐ **TUE**

☐ **WED**

☐ **THU**

☐ **FRI**

☐ **SAT**

☐ **SUN**

WEEKLY PLANNER

YEAR

MONTH

WEEK
34

☐ MON

☐ TUE

☐ WED

☐ THU

☐ FRI

☐ SAT

☐ SUN

WEEKLY PLANNER

WEEK
35

MONTH

YEAR

☐
MON

☐
TUE

☐
WED

☐
THU

☐
FRI

☐
SAT

☐
SUN

WEEKLY PLANNER

YEAR

MONTH

WEEK
36

MON

TUE

WED

THU

FRI

SAT

SUN

WEEKLY PLANNER

WEEK
37

MONTH

YEAR

☐
MON

☐
TUE

☐
WED

☐
THU

☐
FRI

☐
SAT

☐
SUN

WEEKLY PLANNER

YEAR

MONTH

WEEK
38

☐ MON

☐ TUE

☐ WED

☐ THU

☐ FRI

☐ SAT

☐ SUN

WEEKLY PLANNER

WEEK
39

MONTH

YEAR

☐
MON

☐
TUE

☐
WED

☐
THU

☐
FRI

☐
SAT

☐
SUN

WEEKLY PLANNER

YEAR

MONTH

WEEK
40

□ MON

□ TUE

□ WED

□ THU

□ FRI

□ SAT

□ SUN

WEEKLY PLANNER

WEEK
41

MONTH

YEAR

☐ **MON**

☐ **TUE**

☐ **WED**

☐ **THU**

☐ **FRI**

☐ **SAT**

☐ **SUN**

WEEKLY PLANNER

YEAR

MONTH

WEEK
42

☐
MON

☐
TUE

☐
WED

☐
THU

☐
FRI

☐
SAT

☐
SUN

WEEKLY PLANNER

WEEK
43

MONTH

YEAR

☐ **MON**

☐ **TUE**

☐ **WED**

☐ **THU**

☐ **FRI**

☐ **SAT**

☐ **SUN**

WEEKLY PLANNER

YEAR

MONTH

WEEK
44

☐ **MON**

☐ **TUE**

☐ **WED**

☐ **THU**

☐ **FRI**

☐ **SAT**

☐ **SUN**

WEEKLY PLANNER

WEEK
45

MONTH

YEAR

☐ **MON**

☐ **TUE**

☐ **WED**

☐ **THU**

☐ **FRI**

☐ **SAT**

☐ **SUN**

WEEKLY PLANNER

YEAR

MONTH

WEEK
46

☐ **MON**

☐ **TUE**

☐ **WED**

☐ **THU**

☐ **FRI**

☐ **SAT**

☐ **SUN**

WEEKLY PLANNER

WEEK
47

MONTH

YEAR

☐
MON

☐
TUE

☐
WED

☐
THU

☐
FRI

☐
SAT

☐
SUN

WEEKLY PLANNER

YEAR

MONTH

WEEK
48

☐ **MON**

☐ **TUE**

☐ **WED**

☐ **THU**

☐ **FRI**

☐ **SAT**

☐ **SUN**

WEEKLY PLANNER

WEEK
49

MONTH

YEAR

☐ **MON**

☐ **TUE**

☐ **WED**

☐ **THU**

☐ **FRI**

☐ **SAT**

☐ **SUN**

WEEKLY PLANNER

YEAR

MONTH

WEEK
50

☐ MON

☐ TUE

☐ WED

☐ THU

☐ FRI

☐ SAT

☐ SUN

WEEKLY PLANNER

WEEK
51

MONTH

YEAR

☐ **MON**

☐ **TUE**

☐ **WED**

☐ **THU**

☐ **FRI**

☐ **SAT**

☐ **SUN**

WEEKLY PLANNER

YEAR

MONTH

WEEK
52

☐ **MON**

☐ **TUE**

☐ **WED**

☐ **THU**

☐ **FRI**

☐ **SAT**

☐ **SUN**

WEEKLY PLANNER

WEEK

MONTH

YEAR

☐ **MON**

☐ **TUE**

☐ **WED**

☐ **THU**

☐ **FRI**

☐ **SAT**

☐ **SUN**

WEEKLY PLANNER

YEAR

MONTH

WEEK

☐ MON

☐ TUE

☐ WED

☐ THU

☐ FRI

☐ SAT

☐ SUN

WEEKLY PLANNER

WEEK

MONTH

YEAR

MON

TUE

WED

THU

FRI

SAT

SUN

WEEKLY PLANNER

YEAR

MONTH

WEEK

MON

TUE

WED

THU

FRI

SAT

SUN

DAILY PLANNER

Date: ___/___/____ m t w t f s s

Appointments

05:00	
05:30	
06:00	
06:30	
07:00	
07:30	
08:00	
08:30	
09:00	
09:30	
10:00	
10:30	
11:00	
11:30	
12:00	
12:30	
13:00	
13:30	
14:00	
14:30	
15:00	
15:30	
16:00	
16:30	
17:00	
17:30	
18:00	
18:30	
19:00	
19:30	
20:00	
20:30	
21:00	
21:30	
22:00	
22:30	
23:00	
23:30	
24:00	

TODAY GOAL

IMPORTANT TASKS

- [ ]
- [ ]
- [ ]
- [ ]

MEAL TRACKER

WATER

FRUIT / VEGETABLE

EXERCISE

NOTES

DAILY PLANNER

m t w t f s s   Date: ___ / ___ / ___

TODAY GOAL

IMPORTANT TASKS

☐
☐
☐
☐

MEAL TRACKER

WATER

FRUIT / VEGETABLE

EXERCISE

NOTES

Appointments

05:00 _____
05:30 _____
06:00 _____
06:30 _____
07:00 _____
07:30 _____
08:00 _____
08:30 _____
09:00 _____
09:30 _____
10:00 _____
10:30 _____
11:00 _____
11:30 _____
12:00 _____
12:30 _____
13:00 _____
13:30 _____
14:00 _____
14:30 _____
15:00 _____
15:30 _____
16:00 _____
16:30 _____
17:00 _____
17:30 _____
18:00 _____
18:30 _____
19:00 _____
19:30 _____
20:00 _____
20:30 _____
21:00 _____
21:30 _____
22:00 _____
22:30 _____
23:00 _____
23:30 _____
24:00 _____

DAILY PLANNER

Date: ___/___/____ m t w t f s s

Appointments

05:00 _____
05:30 _____
06:00 _____
06:30 _____
07:00 _____
07:30 _____
08:00 _____
08:30 _____
09:00 _____
09:30 _____
10:00 _____
10:30 _____
11:00 _____
11:30 _____
12:00 _____
12:30 _____
13:00 _____
13:30 _____
14:00 _____
14:30 _____
15:00 _____
15:30 _____
16:00 _____
16:30 _____
17:00 _____
17:30 _____
18:00 _____
18:30 _____
19:00 _____
19:30 _____
20:00 _____
20:30 _____
21:00 _____
21:30 _____
22:00 _____
22:30 _____
23:00 _____
23:30 _____
24:00 _____

TODAY GOAL

IMPORTANT TASKS

☐ _____
☐ _____
☐ _____
☐ _____

MEAL TRACKER

WATER

FRUIT / VEGETABLE

EXERCISE

NOTES

126

DAILY PLANNER

m t w t f s s   Date: ___ / ___ / ___

TODAY GOAL	Appointments
	05:00 _____

TODAY GOAL

IMPORTANT TASKS

☐ _____

☐ _____

☐ _____

☐ _____

MEAL TRACKER

WATER

FRUIT / VEGETABLE

EXERCISE

NOTES

Appointments

05:00 _____
05:30 _____
06:00 _____
06:30 _____
07:00 _____
07:30 _____
08:00 _____
08:30 _____
09:00 _____
09:30 _____
10:00 _____
10:30 _____
11:00 _____
11:30 _____
12:00 _____
12:30 _____
13:00 _____
13:30 _____
14:00 _____
14:30 _____
15:00 _____
15:30 _____
16:00 _____
16:30 _____
17:00 _____
17:30 _____
18:00 _____
18:30 _____
19:00 _____
19:30 _____
20:00 _____
20:30 _____
21:00 _____
21:30 _____
22:00 _____
22:30 _____
23:00 _____
23:30 _____
24:00 _____

DAILY PLANNER

Date: ___ / ___ / ___   m t w t f s s

Appointments

05:00 _____
05:30 _____
06:00 _____
06:30 _____
07:00 _____
07:30 _____
08:00 _____
08:30 _____
09:00 _____
09:30 _____
10:00 _____
10:30 _____
11:00 _____
11:30 _____
12:00 _____
12:30 _____
13:00 _____
13:30 _____
14:00 _____
14:30 _____
15:00 _____
15:30 _____
16:00 _____
16:30 _____
17:00 _____
17:30 _____
18:00 _____
18:30 _____
19:00 _____
19:30 _____
20:00 _____
20:30 _____
21:00 _____
21:30 _____
22:00 _____
22:30 _____
23:00 _____
23:30 _____
24:00 _____

TODAY GOAL

IMPORTANT TASKS

- [ ] ....
- [ ] ....
- [ ] ....
- [ ] ....

MEAL TRACKER

WATER

FRUIT / VEGETABLE

EXERCISE

NOTES

DAILY PLANNER

m t w t f s s   Date: ___ / ___ / ___

TODAY GOAL

IMPORTANT TASKS

☐ ---------------------------------
☐ ---------------------------------
☐ ---------------------------------
☐ ---------------------------------

MEAL TRACKER

WATER

FRUIT / VEGETABLE

EXERCISE

NOTES

Appointments	
05:00	
05:30	
06:00	
06:30	
07:00	
07:30	
08:00	
08:30	
09:00	
09:30	
10:00	
10:30	
11:00	
11:30	
12:00	
12:30	
13:00	
13:30	
14:00	
14:30	
15:00	
15:30	
16:00	
16:30	
17:00	
17:30	
18:00	
18:30	
19:00	
19:30	
20:00	
20:30	
21:00	
21:30	
22:00	
22:30	
23:00	
23:30	
24:00	

DAILY PLANNER

Date: ___ / ___ / ___ (m)(t)(w)(t)(f)(s)(s)

Appointments

05:00 _____
05:30 _____
06:00 _____
06:30 _____
07:00 _____
07:30 _____
08:00 _____
08:30 _____
09:00 _____
09:30 _____
10:00 _____
10:30 _____
11:00 _____
11:30 _____
12:00 _____
12:30 _____
13:00 _____
13:30 _____
14:00 _____
14:30 _____
15:00 _____
15:30 _____
16:00 _____
16:30 _____
17:00 _____
17:30 _____
18:00 _____
18:30 _____
19:00 _____
19:30 _____
20:00 _____
20:30 _____
21:00 _____
21:30 _____
22:00 _____
22:30 _____
23:00 _____
23:30 _____
24:00 _____

TODAY GOAL

IMPORTANT TASKS

☐ _____
☐ _____
☐ _____
☐ _____

MEAL TRACKER

WATER

FRUIT / VEGETABLE

EXERCISE

NOTES

130

DAILY PLANNER

m t w t f s s Date: ___ / ___ / ___

TODAY GOAL	Appointments

TODAY GOAL

IMPORTANT TASKS

☐
☐
☐
☐

MEAL TRACKER

WATER

FRUIT / VEGETABLE

EXERCISE

NOTES

Appointments

05:00
05:30
06:00
06:30
07:00
07:30
08:00
08:30
09:00
09:30
10:00
10:30
11:00
11:30
12:00
12:30
13:00
13:30
14:00
14:30
15:00
15:30
16:00
16:30
17:00
17:30
18:00
18:30
19:00
19:30
20:00
20:30
21:00
21:30
22:00
22:30
23:00
23:30
24:00

131

DAILY PLANNER

Date: ___ / ___ / ____ (m) (t) (w) (t) (f) (s) (s)

Appointments

05:00	
05:30	
06:00	
06:30	
07:00	
07:30	
08:00	
08:30	
09:00	
09:30	
10:00	
10:30	
11:00	
11:30	
12:00	
12:30	
13:00	
13:30	
14:00	
14:30	
15:00	
15:30	
16:00	
16:30	
17:00	
17:30	
18:00	
18:30	
19:00	
19:30	
20:00	
20:30	
21:00	
21:30	
22:00	
22:30	
23:00	
23:30	
24:00	

TODAY GOAL

IMPORTANT TASKS

☐
☐
☐
☐

MEAL TRACKER

WATER

FRUIT / VEGETABLE

EXERCISE

NOTES

DAILY PLANNER

m t w t f s s   Date: ___ / ___ / ____

TODAY GOAL

IMPORTANT TASKS

☐ --

☐ --

☐ --

☐ --

MEAL TRACKER

WATER

FRUIT / VEGETABLE

EXERCISE

NOTES

Time	
05:00	_____
05:30	_____
06:00	_____
06:30	_____
07:00	_____
07:30	_____
08:00	_____
08:30	_____
09:00	_____
09:30	_____
10:00	_____
10:30	_____
11:00	_____
11:30	_____
12:00	_____
12:30	_____
13:00	_____
13:30	_____
14:00	_____
14:30	_____
15:00	_____
15:30	_____
16:00	_____
16:30	_____
17:00	_____
17:30	_____
18:00	_____
18:30	_____
19:00	_____
19:30	_____
20:00	_____
20:30	_____
21:00	_____
21:30	_____
22:00	_____
22:30	_____
23:00	_____
23:30	_____
24:00	_____

DAILY PLANNER

Date: ___ / ___ / ___   m t w t f s s

Appointments

05:00	
05:30	
06:00	
06:30	
07:00	
07:30	
08:00	
08:30	
09:00	
09:30	
10:00	
10:30	
11:00	
11:30	
12:00	
12:30	
13:00	
13:30	
14:00	
14:30	
15:00	
15:30	
16:00	
16:30	
17:00	
17:30	
18:00	
18:30	
19:00	
19:30	
20:00	
20:30	
21:00	
21:30	
22:00	
22:30	
23:00	
23:30	
24:00	

TODAY GOAL

IMPORTANT TASKS

☐
☐
☐
☐

MEAL TRACKER

WATER

FRUIT / VEGETABLE

EXERCISE

NOTES

134

DAILY PLANNER

m t w t f s s

Appointments

TODAY GOAL	05:00 _____
	05:30 _____
	06:00 _____
	06:30 _____
IMPORTANT TASKS	07:00 _____
☐	07:30 _____
☐	08:00 _____
☐	08:30 _____
☐	09:00 _____
☐	09:30 _____
MEAL TRACKER	10:00 _____
	10:30 _____
	11:00 _____
	11:30 _____
	12:00 _____
	12:30 _____
	13:00 _____
WATER	13:30 _____
	14:00 _____
	14:30 _____
FRUIT / VEGETABLE	15:00 _____
	15:30 _____
	16:00 _____
	16:30 _____
EXERCISE	17:00 _____
	17:30 _____
	18:00 _____
	18:30 _____
	19:00 _____
	19:30 _____
	20:00 _____
NOTES	20:30 _____
	21:00 _____
	21:30 _____
	22:00 _____
	22:30 _____
	23:00 _____
	23:30 _____
	24:00 _____

DAILY PLANNER

Date: ___/___/____ (m) (t) (w) (t) (f) (s) (s)

Appointments

05:00	
05:30	
06:00	
06:30	
07:00	
07:30	
08:00	
08:30	
09:00	
09:30	
10:00	
10:30	
11:00	
11:30	
12:00	
12:30	
13:00	
13:30	
14:00	
14:30	
15:00	
15:30	
16:00	
16:30	
17:00	
17:30	
18:00	
18:30	
19:00	
19:30	
20:00	
20:30	
21:00	
21:30	
22:00	
22:30	
23:00	
23:30	
24:00	

TODAY GOAL

IMPORTANT TASKS

☐
☐
☐
☐

MEAL TRACKER

WATER

FRUIT / VEGETABLE

EXERCISE

NOTES

DAILY PLANNER

(m) (t) (w) (t) (f) (s) (s)   Date: ___ / ___ / ____

TODAY GOAL

IMPORTANT TASKS

☐ ------------------------------------

☐ ------------------------------------

☐ ------------------------------------

☐ ------------------------------------

MEAL TRACKER

WATER

FRUIT / VEGETABLE

EXERCISE

NOTES

05:00 _____
05:30 _____
06:00 _____
06:30 _____
07:00 _____
07:30 _____
08:00 _____
08:30 _____
09:00 _____
09:30 _____
10:00 _____
10:30 _____
11:00 _____
11:30 _____
12:00 _____
12:30 _____
13:00 _____
13:30 _____
14:00 _____
14:30 _____
15:00 _____
15:30 _____
16:00 _____
16:30 _____
17:00 _____
17:30 _____
18:00 _____
18:30 _____
19:00 _____
19:30 _____
20:00 _____
20:30 _____
21:00 _____
21:30 _____
22:00 _____
22:30 _____
23:00 _____
23:30 _____
24:00 _____

DAILY PLANNER

Date: ___/___/____ m t w t f s s

Appointments

Time	
05:00	
05:30	
06:00	
06:30	
07:00	
07:30	
08:00	
08:30	
09:00	
09:30	
10:00	
10:30	
11:00	
11:30	
12:00	
12:30	
13:00	
13:30	
14:00	
14:30	
15:00	
15:30	
16:00	
16:30	
17:00	
17:30	
18:00	
18:30	
19:00	
19:30	
20:00	
20:30	
21:00	
21:30	
22:00	
22:30	
23:00	
23:30	
24:00	

TODAY GOAL

IMPORTANT TASKS

- [ ]
- [ ]
- [ ]
- [ ]

MEAL TRACKER

WATER

FRUIT / VEGETABLE

EXERCISE

NOTES

DAILY PLANNER

m t w t f s s   Date: ___ / ___ / ____

TODAY GOAL

IMPORTANT TASKS

☐ ------------------------------------

☐ ------------------------------------

☐ ------------------------------------

☐ ------------------------------------

MEAL TRACKER

WATER

FRUIT / VEGETABLE

EXERCISE

NOTES

Appointments

05:00 ----------------
05:30 ----------------
06:00 ----------------
06:30 ----------------
07:00 ----------------
07:30 ----------------
08:00 ----------------
08:30 ----------------
09:00 ----------------
09:30 ----------------
10:00 ----------------
10:30 ----------------
11:00 ----------------
11:30 ----------------
12:00 ----------------
12:30 ----------------
13:00 ----------------
13:30 ----------------
14:00 ----------------
14:30 ----------------
15:00 ----------------
15:30 ----------------
16:00 ----------------
16:30 ----------------
17:00 ----------------
17:30 ----------------
18:00 ----------------
18:30 ----------------
19:00 ----------------
19:30 ----------------
20:00 ----------------
20:30 ----------------
21:00 ----------------
21:30 ----------------
22:00 ----------------
22:30 ----------------
23:00 ----------------
23:30 ----------------
24:00 ----------------

DAILY PLANNER

Date: ___ / ___ / ____ (m) (t) (w) (t) (f) (s) (s)

Appointments

Time	
05:00	
05:30	
06:00	
06:30	
07:00	
07:30	
08:00	
08:30	
09:00	
09:30	
10:00	
10:30	
11:00	
11:30	
12:00	
12:30	
13:00	
13:30	
14:00	
14:30	
15:00	
15:30	
16:00	
16:30	
17:00	
17:30	
18:00	
18:30	
19:00	
19:30	
20:00	
20:30	
21:00	
21:30	
22:00	
22:30	
23:00	
23:30	
24:00	

TODAY GOAL

IMPORTANT TASKS

- ☐
- ☐
- ☐
- ☐

MEAL TRACKER

WATER

FRUIT / VEGETABLE

EXERCISE

NOTES

140

DAILY PLANNER

m t w t f s s Date: ___ / ___ / ____

TODAY GOAL	Appointments
	05:00 _____

TODAY GOAL

IMPORTANT TASKS

☐ ....
☐ ....
☐ ....
☐ ....

MEAL TRACKER

WATER

FRUIT / VEGETABLE

EXERCISE

NOTES

Appointments

05:00 _____
05:30 _____
06:00 _____
06:30 _____
07:00 _____
07:30 _____
08:00 _____
08:30 _____
09:00 _____
09:30 _____
10:00 _____
10:30 _____
11:00 _____
11:30 _____
12:00 _____
12:30 _____
13:00 _____
13:30 _____
14:00 _____
14:30 _____
15:00 _____
15:30 _____
16:00 _____
16:30 _____
17:00 _____
17:30 _____
18:00 _____
18:30 _____
19:00 _____
19:30 _____
20:00 _____
20:30 _____
21:00 _____
21:30 _____
22:00 _____
22:30 _____
23:00 _____
23:30 _____
24:00 _____

DAILY PLANNER

Date: ___/___/____ (m) (t) (w) (t) (f) (s) (s)

Appointments

05:00	------------------
05:30	------------------
06:00	------------------
06:30	------------------
07:00	------------------
07:30	------------------
08:00	------------------
08:30	------------------
09:00	------------------
09:30	------------------
10:00	------------------
10:30	------------------
11:00	------------------
11:30	------------------
12:00	------------------
12:30	------------------
13:00	------------------
13:30	------------------
14:00	------------------
14:30	------------------
15:00	------------------
15:30	------------------
16:00	------------------
16:30	------------------
17:00	------------------
17:30	------------------
18:00	------------------
18:30	------------------
19:00	------------------
19:30	------------------
20:00	------------------
20:30	------------------
21:00	------------------
21:30	------------------
22:00	------------------
22:30	------------------
23:00	------------------
23:30	------------------
24:00	------------------

TODAY GOAL

IMPORTANT TASKS

☐ --
☐ --
☐ --
☐ --

MEAL TRACKER

WATER

FRUIT / VEGETABLE

EXERCISE

NOTES

142

DAILY PLANNER

(m) (t) (w) (t) (f) (s) (s)   Date: ___ / ___ / ___

TODAY GOAL

IMPORTANT TASKS
☐
☐
☐
☐

MEAL TRACKER

WATER

FRUIT / VEGETABLE

EXERCISE

NOTES

Appointments

05:00 _____
05:30 _____
06:00 _____
06:30 _____
07:00 _____
07:30 _____
08:00 _____
08:30 _____
09:00 _____
09:30 _____
10:00 _____
10:30 _____
11:00 _____
11:30 _____
12:00 _____
12:30 _____
13:00 _____
13:30 _____
14:00 _____
14:30 _____
15:00 _____
15:30 _____
16:00 _____
16:30 _____
17:00 _____
17:30 _____
18:00 _____
18:30 _____
19:00 _____
19:30 _____
20:00 _____
20:30 _____
21:00 _____
21:30 _____
22:00 _____
22:30 _____
23:00 _____
23:30 _____
24:00 _____

143

DAILY PLANNER

Date: ___/___/____ (m)(t)(w)(t)(f)(s)(s)

Appointments

05:00	
05:30	
06:00	
06:30	
07:00	
07:30	
08:00	
08:30	
09:00	
09:30	
10:00	
10:30	
11:00	
11:30	
12:00	
12:30	
13:00	
13:30	
14:00	
14:30	
15:00	
15:30	
16:00	
16:30	
17:00	
17:30	
18:00	
18:30	
19:00	
19:30	
20:00	
20:30	
21:00	
21:30	
22:00	
22:30	
23:00	
23:30	
24:00	

TODAY GOAL

IMPORTANT TASKS

☐
☐
☐
☐

MEAL TRACKER

WATER

FRUIT / VEGETABLE

EXERCISE

NOTES

DAILY PLANNER

m t w t f s s Date: ___/___/____

TODAY GOAL

IMPORTANT TASKS

- [ ]
- [ ]
- [ ]
- [ ]

MEAL TRACKER

WATER

FRUIT / VEGETABLE

EXERCISE

NOTES

Time	Appointments
05:00	
05:30	
06:00	
06:30	
07:00	
07:30	
08:00	
08:30	
09:00	
09:30	
10:00	
10:30	
11:00	
11:30	
12:00	
12:30	
13:00	
13:30	
14:00	
14:30	
15:00	
15:30	
16:00	
16:30	
17:00	
17:30	
18:00	
18:30	
19:00	
19:30	
20:00	
20:30	
21:00	
21:30	
22:00	
22:30	
23:00	
23:30	
24:00	

DAILY PLANNER

Date: ___ / ___ / ___   (m) (t) (w) (t) (f) (s) (s)

Appointments

Time	
05:00	
05:30	
06:00	
06:30	
07:00	
07:30	
08:00	
08:30	
09:00	
09:30	
10:00	
10:30	
11:00	
11:30	
12:00	
12:30	
13:00	
13:30	
14:00	
14:30	
15:00	
15:30	
16:00	
16:30	
17:00	
17:30	
18:00	
18:30	
19:00	
19:30	
20:00	
20:30	
21:00	
21:30	
22:00	
22:30	
23:00	
23:30	
24:00	

TODAY GOAL

IMPORTANT TASKS

☐

☐

☐

☐

MEAL TRACKER

WATER

FRUIT / VEGETABLE

EXERCISE

NOTES

DAILY PLANNER

m t w t f s s   Date: ___ / ___ / ____

TODAY GOAL

IMPORTANT TASKS

☐ ------------------------------------
☐ ------------------------------------
☐ ------------------------------------
☐ ------------------------------------

MEAL TRACKER

WATER

FRUIT / VEGETABLE

EXERCISE

NOTES

	Appointments
05:00	_____
05:30	_____
06:00	_____
06:30	_____
07:00	_____
07:30	_____
08:00	_____
08:30	_____
09:00	_____
09:30	_____
10:00	_____
10:30	_____
11:00	_____
11:30	_____
12:00	_____
12:30	_____
13:00	_____
13:30	_____
14:00	_____
14:30	_____
15:00	_____
15:30	_____
16:00	_____
16:30	_____
17:00	_____
17:30	_____
18:00	_____
18:30	_____
19:00	_____
19:30	_____
20:00	_____
20:30	_____
21:00	_____
21:30	_____
22:00	_____
22:30	_____
23:00	_____
23:30	_____
24:00	_____

DAILY PLANNER

Date: ___ / ___ / ____ m t w t f s s

Appointments

05:00	
05:30	
06:00	
06:30	
07:00	
07:30	
08:00	
08:30	
09:00	
09:30	
10:00	
10:30	
11:00	
11:30	
12:00	
12:30	
13:00	
13:30	
14:00	
14:30	
15:00	
15:30	
16:00	
16:30	
17:00	
17:30	
18:00	
18:30	
19:00	
19:30	
20:00	
20:30	
21:00	
21:30	
22:00	
22:30	
23:00	
23:30	
24:00	

TODAY GOAL

IMPORTANT TASKS

- ☐
- ☐
- ☐
- ☐

MEAL TRACKER

WATER

FRUIT / VEGETABLE

EXERCISE

NOTES

DAILY PLANNER

m t w t f s s   Date: ___ / ___ / ____

TODAY GOAL

IMPORTANT TASKS

☐ ---
☐ ---
☐ ---
☐ ---

MEAL TRACKER

WATER

FRUIT / VEGETABLE

EXERCISE

NOTES

Appointments

05:00 _____
05:30 _____
06:00 _____
06:30 _____
07:00 _____
07:30 _____
08:00 _____
08:30 _____
09:00 _____
09:30 _____
10:00 _____
10:30 _____
11:00 _____
11:30 _____
12:00 _____
12:30 _____
13:00 _____
13:30 _____
14:00 _____
14:30 _____
15:00 _____
15:30 _____
16:00 _____
16:30 _____
17:00 _____
17:30 _____
18:00 _____
18:30 _____
19:00 _____
19:30 _____
20:00 _____
20:30 _____
21:00 _____
21:30 _____
22:00 _____
22:30 _____
23:00 _____
23:30 _____
24:00 _____

DAILY PLANNER

Date: ___/___/____ m t w t f s s

Appointments

Time	
05:00	
05:30	
06:00	
06:30	
07:00	
07:30	
08:00	
08:30	
09:00	
09:30	
10:00	
10:30	
11:00	
11:30	
12:00	
12:30	
13:00	
13:30	
14:00	
14:30	
15:00	
15:30	
16:00	
16:30	
17:00	
17:30	
18:00	
18:30	
19:00	
19:30	
20:00	
20:30	
21:00	
21:30	
22:00	
22:30	
23:00	
23:30	
24:00	

TODAY GOAL

IMPORTANT TASKS

☐
☐
☐
☐

MEAL TRACKER

WATER

FRUIT / VEGETABLE

EXERCISE

NOTES

DAILY PLANNER

m t w t f s s   Date: ___ / ___ / ___

TODAY GOAL

IMPORTANT TASKS

- [ ]
- [ ]
- [ ]
- [ ]

MEAL TRACKER

WATER

FRUIT / VEGETABLE

EXERCISE

NOTES

Appointments

05:00 _____
05:30 _____
06:00 _____
06:30 _____
07:00 _____
07:30 _____
08:00 _____
08:30 _____
09:00 _____
09:30 _____
10:00 _____
10:30 _____
11:00 _____
11:30 _____
12:00 _____
12:30 _____
13:00 _____
13:30 _____
14:00 _____
14:30 _____
15:00 _____
15:30 _____
16:00 _____
16:30 _____
17:00 _____
17:30 _____
18:00 _____
18:30 _____
19:00 _____
19:30 _____
20:00 _____
20:30 _____
21:00 _____
21:30 _____
22:00 _____
22:30 _____
23:00 _____
23:30 _____
24:00 _____

DAILY PLANNER

Date: ___/___/____ (m)(t)(w)(t)(f)(s)(s)

Appointments

05:00	
05:30	
06:00	
06:30	
07:00	
07:30	
08:00	
08:30	
09:00	
09:30	
10:00	
10:30	
11:00	
11:30	
12:00	
12:30	
13:00	
13:30	
14:00	
14:30	
15:00	
15:30	
16:00	
16:30	
17:00	
17:30	
18:00	
18:30	
19:00	
19:30	
20:00	
20:30	
21:00	
21:30	
22:00	
22:30	
23:00	
23:30	
24:00	

TODAY GOAL

IMPORTANT TASKS

☐
☐
☐
☐

MEAL TRACKER

WATER

FRUIT / VEGETABLE

EXERCISE

NOTES

152

DAILY PLANNER

(m) (t) (w) (t) (f) (s) (s)   Date: ___ / ___ / ___

TODAY GOAL

IMPORTANT TASKS

- [ ]
- [ ]
- [ ]
- [ ]

MEAL TRACKER

WATER

FRUIT / VEGETABLE

EXERCISE

NOTES

Appointments

05:00 _____
05:30 _____
06:00 _____
06:30 _____
07:00 _____
07:30 _____
08:00 _____
08:30 _____
09:00 _____
09:30 _____
10:00 _____
10:30 _____
11:00 _____
11:30 _____
12:00 _____
12:30 _____
13:00 _____
13:30 _____
14:00 _____
14:30 _____
15:00 _____
15:30 _____
16:00 _____
16:30 _____
17:00 _____
17:30 _____
18:00 _____
18:30 _____
19:00 _____
19:30 _____
20:00 _____
20:30 _____
21:00 _____
21:30 _____
22:00 _____
22:30 _____
23:00 _____
23:30 _____
24:00 _____

DAILY PLANNER

Date: ___ / ___ / ____ (m) (t) (w) (t) (f) (s) (s)

Appointments

05:00	_____
05:30	_____
06:00	_____
06:30	_____
07:00	_____
07:30	_____
08:00	_____
08:30	_____
09:00	_____
09:30	_____
10:00	_____
10:30	_____
11:00	_____
11:30	_____
12:00	_____
12:30	_____
13:00	_____
13:30	_____
14:00	_____
14:30	_____
15:00	_____
15:30	_____
16:00	_____
16:30	_____
17:00	_____
17:30	_____
18:00	_____
18:30	_____
19:00	_____
19:30	_____
20:00	_____
20:30	_____
21:00	_____
21:30	_____
22:00	_____
22:30	_____
23:00	_____
23:30	_____
24:00	_____

TODAY GOAL

IMPORTANT TASKS

☐ _____
☐ _____
☐ _____
☐ _____

MEAL TRACKER

WATER

FRUIT / VEGETABLE

EXERCISE

NOTES

DAILY PLANNER

(m) (t) (w) (t) (f) (s) (s)   Date: ___/___/____

TODAY GOAL

IMPORTANT TASKS

☐ --
☐ --
☐ --
☐

MEAL TRACKER

WATER

FRUIT / VEGETABLE

EXERCISE

NOTES

Appointments

05:00 ----------------
05:30 ----------------
06:00 ----------------
06:30 ----------------
07:00 ----------------
07:30 ----------------
08:00 ----------------
08:30 ----------------
09:00 ----------------
09:30 ----------------
10:00 ----------------
10:30 ----------------
11:00 ----------------
11:30 ----------------
12:00 ----------------
12:30 ----------------
13:00 ----------------
13:30 ----------------
14:00 ----------------
14:30 ----------------
15:00 ----------------
15:30 ----------------
16:00 ----------------
16:30 ----------------
17:00 ----------------
17:30 ----------------
18:00 ----------------
18:30 ----------------
19:00 ----------------
19:30 ----------------
20:00 ----------------
20:30 ----------------
21:00 ----------------
21:30 ----------------
22:00 ----------------
22:30 ----------------
23:00 ----------------
23:30 ----------------
24:00 ----------------

DAILY PLANNER

Date: ___/___/_____ m t w t f s s

Appointments

Time	
05:00	
05:30	
06:00	
06:30	
07:00	
07:30	
08:00	
08:30	
09:00	
09:30	
10:00	
10:30	
11:00	
11:30	
12:00	
12:30	
13:00	
13:30	
14:00	
14:30	
15:00	
15:30	
16:00	
16:30	
17:00	
17:30	
18:00	
18:30	
19:00	
19:30	
20:00	
20:30	
21:00	
21:30	
22:00	
22:30	
23:00	
23:30	
24:00	

TODAY GOAL

IMPORTANT TASKS

☐
☐
☐
☐

MEAL TRACKER

WATER

FRUIT / VEGETABLE

EXERCISE

NOTES

DAILY PLANNER

m t w t f s s   Date: ___ / ___ / ___

TODAY GOAL

IMPORTANT TASKS

☐ ------------------------------------
☐ ------------------------------------
☐ ------------------------------------
☐ ------------------------------------

MEAL TRACKER

WATER

FRUIT / VEGETABLE

EXERCISE

NOTES

05:00	_____
05:30	_____
06:00	_____
06:30	_____
07:00	_____
07:30	_____
08:00	_____
08:30	_____
09:00	_____
09:30	_____
10:00	_____
10:30	_____
11:00	_____
11:30	_____
12:00	_____
12:30	_____
13:00	_____
13:30	_____
14:00	_____
14:30	_____
15:00	_____
15:30	_____
16:00	_____
16:30	_____
17:00	_____
17:30	_____
18:00	_____
18:30	_____
19:00	_____
19:30	_____
20:00	_____
20:30	_____
21:00	_____
21:30	_____
22:00	_____
22:30	_____
23:00	_____
23:30	_____
24:00	_____

DAILY PLANNER

Date: ___/___/____ m t w t f s s

Appointments

05:00 _____
05:30 _____
06:00 _____
06:30 _____
07:00 _____
07:30 _____
08:00 _____
08:30 _____
09:00 _____
09:30 _____
10:00 _____
10:30 _____
11:00 _____
11:30 _____
12:00 _____
12:30 _____
13:00 _____
13:30 _____
14:00 _____
14:30 _____
15:00 _____
15:30 _____
16:00 _____
16:30 _____
17:00 _____
17:30 _____
18:00 _____
18:30 _____
19:00 _____
19:30 _____
20:00 _____
20:30 _____
21:00 _____
21:30 _____
22:00 _____
22:30 _____
23:00 _____
23:30 _____
24:00 _____

TODAY GOAL

IMPORTANT TASKS

☐ _____
☐ _____
☐ _____
☐ _____

MEAL TRACKER

WATER

FRUIT / VEGETABLE

EXERCISE

NOTES

158

DAILY PLANNER

m t w t f s s   Date: ___ / ___ / ____

TODAY GOAL

IMPORTANT TASKS

☐ ---

☐ ---

☐ ---

☐ ---

MEAL TRACKER

WATER

FRUIT / VEGETABLE

EXERCISE

NOTES

Appointments

05:00 ----------------
05:30 ----------------
06:00 ----------------
06:30 ----------------
07:00 ----------------
07:30 ----------------
08:00 ----------------
08:30 ----------------
09:00 ----------------
09:30 ----------------
10:00 ----------------
10:30 ----------------
11:00 ----------------
11:30 ----------------
12:00 ----------------
12:30 ----------------
13:00 ----------------
13:30 ----------------
14:00 ----------------
14:30 ----------------
15:00 ----------------
15:30 ----------------
16:00 ----------------
16:30 ----------------
17:00 ----------------
17:30 ----------------
18:00 ----------------
18:30 ----------------
19:00 ----------------
19:30 ----------------
20:00 ----------------
20:30 ----------------
21:00 ----------------
21:30 ----------------
22:00 ----------------
22:30 ----------------
23:00 ----------------
23:30 ----------------
24:00 ----------------

DAILY PLANNER

Date: ___ / ___ / ____ (m) (t) (w) (t) (f) (s) (s)

Appointments

Time	
05:00	
05:30	
06:00	
06:30	
07:00	
07:30	
08:00	
08:30	
09:00	
09:30	
10:00	
10:30	
11:00	
11:30	
12:00	
12:30	
13:00	
13:30	
14:00	
14:30	
15:00	
15:30	
16:00	
16:30	
17:00	
17:30	
18:00	
18:30	
19:00	
19:30	
20:00	
20:30	
21:00	
21:30	
22:00	
22:30	
23:00	
23:30	
24:00	

TODAY GOAL

IMPORTANT TASKS

☐
☐
☐
☐

MEAL TRACKER

WATER

FRUIT / VEGETABLE

EXERCISE

NOTES

DAILY PLANNER

m t w t f s s   Date: ___/___/____

TODAY GOAL

IMPORTANT TASKS

- ☐
- ☐
- ☐
- ☐

MEAL TRACKER

WATER

FRUIT / VEGETABLE

EXERCISE

NOTES

Appointments	
05:00	_____
05:30	_____
06:00	_____
06:30	_____
07:00	_____
07:30	_____
08:00	_____
08:30	_____
09:00	_____
09:30	_____
10:00	_____
10:30	_____
11:00	_____
11:30	_____
12:00	_____
12:30	_____
13:00	_____
13:30	_____
14:00	_____
14:30	_____
15:00	_____
15:30	_____
16:00	_____
16:30	_____
17:00	_____
17:30	_____
18:00	_____
18:30	_____
19:00	_____
19:30	_____
20:00	_____
20:30	_____
21:00	_____
21:30	_____
22:00	_____
22:30	_____
23:00	_____
23:30	_____
24:00	_____

DAILY PLANNER

Date: ___ / ___ / ___ (m) (t) (w) (t) (f) (s) (s)

Appointments

Time	
05:00	
05:30	
06:00	
06:30	
07:00	
07:30	
08:00	
08:30	
09:00	
09:30	
10:00	
10:30	
11:00	
11:30	
12:00	
12:30	
13:00	
13:30	
14:00	
14:30	
15:00	
15:30	
16:00	
16:30	
17:00	
17:30	
18:00	
18:30	
19:00	
19:30	
20:00	
20:30	
21:00	
21:30	
22:00	
22:30	
23:00	
23:30	
24:00	

TODAY GOAL

IMPORTANT TASKS

☐
☐
☐
☐

MEAL TRACKER

WATER

FRUIT / VEGETABLE

EXERCISE

NOTES

162

DAILY PLANNER

m t w t f s s Date: ___ / ___ / ____

TODAY GOAL

IMPORTANT TASKS

☐ -------------------------------
☐ -------------------------------
☐ -------------------------------
☐

MEAL TRACKER

WATER

FRUIT / VEGETABLE

EXERCISE

NOTES

Time	
05:00	
05:30	
06:00	
06:30	
07:00	
07:30	
08:00	
08:30	
09:00	
09:30	
10:00	
10:30	
11:00	
11:30	
12:00	
12:30	
13:00	
13:30	
14:00	
14:30	
15:00	
15:30	
16:00	
16:30	
17:00	
17:30	
18:00	
18:30	
19:00	
19:30	
20:00	
20:30	
21:00	
21:30	
22:00	
22:30	
23:00	
23:30	
24:00	

DAILY PLANNER

Date: ___ / ___ / ___   m t w t f s s

Appointments

05:00	
05:30	
06:00	
06:30	
07:00	
07:30	
08:00	
08:30	
09:00	
09:30	
10:00	
10:30	
11:00	
11:30	
12:00	
12:30	
13:00	
13:30	
14:00	
14:30	
15:00	
15:30	
16:00	
16:30	
17:00	
17:30	
18:00	
18:30	
19:00	
19:30	
20:00	
20:30	
21:00	
21:30	
22:00	
22:30	
23:00	
23:30	
24:00	

TODAY GOAL

IMPORTANT TASKS

- [ ]
- [ ]
- [ ]
- [ ]

MEAL TRACKER

WATER

FRUIT / VEGETABLE

EXERCISE

NOTES

164

DAILY PLANNER

m t w t f s s Date: ___ / ___ / ____

TODAY GOAL	Appointments

Appointments

05:00 _____
05:30 _____
06:00 _____
06:30 _____

IMPORTANT TASKS

☐ ------------------------------------

07:00 _____
07:30 _____

☐ ------------------------------------

08:00 _____
08:30 _____

☐ ------------------------------------

09:00 _____
09:30 _____

☐ ------------------------------------

10:00 _____

MEAL TRACKER

10:30 _____
11:00 _____
11:30 _____
12:00 _____
12:30 _____
13:00 _____
13:30 _____

WATER

14:00 _____
14:30 _____
15:00 _____
15:30 _____

FRUIT / VEGETABLE

16:00 _____
16:30 _____
17:00 _____
17:30 _____

EXERCISE

18:00 _____
18:30 _____
19:00 _____
19:30 _____
20:00 _____
20:30 _____
21:00 _____

NOTES

21:30 _____
22:00 _____
22:30 _____
23:00 _____
23:30 _____
24:00 _____

165

DAILY PLANNER

Date: ___ / ___ / ____   (m) (t) (w) (t) (f) (s) (s)

Appointments

05:00	
05:30	
06:00	
06:30	
07:00	
07:30	
08:00	
08:30	
09:00	
09:30	
10:00	
10:30	
11:00	
11:30	
12:00	
12:30	
13:00	
13:30	
14:00	
14:30	
15:00	
15:30	
16:00	
16:30	
17:00	
17:30	
18:00	
18:30	
19:00	
19:30	
20:00	
20:30	
21:00	
21:30	
22:00	
22:30	
23:00	
23:30	
24:00	

TODAY GOAL

IMPORTANT TASKS

☐
☐
☐
☐

MEAL TRACKER

WATER

FRUIT / VEGETABLE

EXERCISE

NOTES

166

DAILY PLANNER

(m) (t) (w) (t) (f) (s) (s) Date: ___ / ___ / ____

TODAY GOAL

IMPORTANT TASKS

- ☐ _____
- ☐ _____
- ☐ _____
- ☐ _____

MEAL TRACKER

WATER

FRUIT / VEGETABLE

EXERCISE

NOTES

05:00 _____
05:30 _____
06:00 _____
06:30 _____
07:00 _____
07:30 _____
08:00 _____
08:30 _____
09:00 _____
09:30 _____
10:00 _____
10:30 _____
11:00 _____
11:30 _____
12:00 _____
12:30 _____
13:00 _____
13:30 _____
14:00 _____
14:30 _____
15:00 _____
15:30 _____
16:00 _____
16:30 _____
17:00 _____
17:30 _____
18:00 _____
18:30 _____
19:00 _____
19:30 _____
20:00 _____
20:30 _____
21:00 _____
21:30 _____
22:00 _____
22:30 _____
23:00 _____
23:30 _____
24:00 _____

DAILY PLANNER

Date: ___ / ___ / ___ m t w t f s s

Appointments

05:00	
05:30	
06:00	
06:30	
07:00	
07:30	
08:00	
08:30	
09:00	
09:30	
10:00	
10:30	
11:00	
11:30	
12:00	
12:30	
13:00	
13:30	
14:00	
14:30	
15:00	
15:30	
16:00	
16:30	
17:00	
17:30	
18:00	
18:30	
19:00	
19:30	
20:00	
20:30	
21:00	
21:30	
22:00	
22:30	
23:00	
23:30	
24:00	

TODAY GOAL

IMPORTANT TASKS

☐
☐
☐
☐

MEAL TRACKER

WATER

FRUIT / VEGETABLE

EXERCISE

NOTES

168

DAILY PLANNER

m t w t f s s   Date: ___/___/____

TODAY GOAL

IMPORTANT TASKS

☐ --
☐ --
☐ --
☐

MEAL TRACKER

WATER

FRUIT / VEGETABLE

EXERCISE

NOTES

05:00 _____
05:30 _____
06:00 _____
06:30 _____
07:00 _____
07:30 _____
08:00 _____
08:30 _____
09:00 _____
09:30 _____
10:00 _____
10:30 _____
11:00 _____
11:30 _____
12:00 _____
12:30 _____
13:00 _____
13:30 _____
14:00 _____
14:30 _____
15:00 _____
15:30 _____
16:00 _____
16:30 _____
17:00 _____
17:30 _____
18:00 _____
18:30 _____
19:00 _____
19:30 _____
20:00 _____
20:30 _____
21:00 _____
21:30 _____
22:00 _____
22:30 _____
23:00 _____
23:30 _____
24:00 _____

DAILY PLANNER

Date: ___/___/____ ⓜ ⓣ ⓦ ⓣ ⓕ ⓢ ⓢ

Appointments

05:00	
05:30	
06:00	
06:30	
07:00	
07:30	
08:00	
08:30	
09:00	
09:30	
10:00	
10:30	
11:00	
11:30	
12:00	
12:30	
13:00	
13:30	
14:00	
14:30	
15:00	
15:30	
16:00	
16:30	
17:00	
17:30	
18:00	
18:30	
19:00	
19:30	
20:00	
20:30	
21:00	
21:30	
22:00	
22:30	
23:00	
23:30	
24:00	

TODAY GOAL

IMPORTANT TASKS

☐
☐
☐
☐

MEAL TRACKER

WATER

FRUIT / VEGETABLE

EXERCISE

NOTES

DAILY PLANNER

(m) (t) (w) (t) (f) (s) (s)   Date: ___ / ___ / ____

TODAY GOAL

IMPORTANT TASKS

- [ ] _____
- [ ] _____
- [ ] _____
- [ ] _____

07:00 _____
07:30 _____
08:00 _____
08:30 _____
09:00 _____
09:30 _____
10:00 _____

MEAL TRACKER

10:30 _____
11:00 _____
11:30 _____
12:00 _____
12:30 _____
13:00 _____

WATER

13:30 _____
14:00 _____
14:30 _____
15:00 _____

FRUIT / VEGETABLE

15:30 _____
16:00 _____
16:30 _____
17:00 _____

EXERCISE

17:30 _____
18:00 _____
18:30 _____
19:00 _____
19:30 _____
20:00 _____
20:30 _____

NOTES

21:00 _____
21:30 _____
22:00 _____
22:30 _____
23:00 _____
23:30 _____
24:00 _____

171

DAILY PLANNER

Date: ___ / ___ / ____ m t w t f s s

Appointments

05:00 _____
05:30 _____
06:00 _____
06:30 _____
07:00 _____
07:30 _____
08:00 _____
08:30 _____
09:00 _____
09:30 _____
10:00 _____
10:30 _____
11:00 _____
11:30 _____
12:00 _____
12:30 _____
13:00 _____
13:30 _____
14:00 _____
14:30 _____
15:00 _____
15:30 _____
16:00 _____
16:30 _____
17:00 _____
17:30 _____
18:00 _____
18:30 _____
19:00 _____
19:30 _____
20:00 _____
20:30 _____
21:00 _____
21:30 _____
22:00 _____
22:30 _____
23:00 _____
23:30 _____
24:00 _____

TODAY GOAL

IMPORTANT TASKS

☐ _____
☐ _____
☐ _____
☐ _____

MEAL TRACKER

WATER

FRUIT / VEGETABLE

EXERCISE

NOTES

DAILY PLANNER

m t w t f s s   Date: ___ / ___ / _____

TODAY GOAL

IMPORTANT TASKS

- ☐ --------------------------------
- ☐ --------------------------------
- ☐ --------------------------------
- ☐ --------------------------------

MEAL TRACKER

WATER

FRUIT / VEGETABLE

EXERCISE

NOTES

Time	
05:00	
05:30	
06:00	
06:30	
07:00	
07:30	
08:00	
08:30	
09:00	
09:30	
10:00	
10:30	
11:00	
11:30	
12:00	
12:30	
13:00	
13:30	
14:00	
14:30	
15:00	
15:30	
16:00	
16:30	
17:00	
17:30	
18:00	
18:30	
19:00	
19:30	
20:00	
20:30	
21:00	
21:30	
22:00	
22:30	
23:00	
23:30	
24:00	

Made in the USA
Monee, IL
16 December 2021

85896735R00120